CLB 1778
© 1987 Colour Library Books Ltd., Guildford, Surrey, England.
© 1987 Illustrations: The Walt Disney Company.
Printed and bound in Barcelona, Spain by Cronion, S.A.
All rights reserved.
1987 edition published by Crescent Books, distributed by Crown Publishers, Inc.
ISBN 0 51762925 9
h g f e d c b a

Walt Disney World®

CRESCENT BOOKS
NEW YORK

Facing page: Mickey leading the band on Main Street, USA. Top: Christmas showtime, (left) King John recognised, and (above) Mickey playing the press photographer.

11

Previous pages: (left) Mickey painted in flowers in front of Main Street Railroad Station, and (right) the famous mouse greeted by an admirer. Facing page: (bottom left) Tinkerbell aloft, and (top and bottom right) Donald and Goofy showing off. Left: Pinnocchio, Jiminy Cricket and friends take a stroll through Fantasyland, and (below) stars of the 3-D musical space fantasy "Captain EO" perform with Disney characters suitably dressed for space travel. Hooter, the little green elephant who sneezes wild musical notes through his flute-like trunk, and the Geex, a shaggy, golden creature with a dual personality and two heads named Idy and Ody, are just two of the colorful band of mythical space characters who support the film's star, Michael Jackson, in his fight against the forces of darkness. Overleaf: photo-call for Snow White and the Seven Dwarfs.

15

Top: Colonial soldiers and (right and facing page top) a fife and drum corps performing on the Promenade outside the colonial-style American Adventure show building, in which Benjamin Franklin (above) appears with Mark Twain (facing page bottom), World Showcase. Overleaf: flowers for Minnie Mouse.

In the EPCOT Center's World Showcase (these pages) are pavilions evoking some of the universally-recognisable images and traditions of various countries. Top left: the Rose and Crown Pub and (above) a Pearly Band in the United Kingdom, (top) a company of players in Italy, (left and facing page top) China, and (facing page bottom) Germany.

Previous pages: (left) the Chinese pagoda, (right top) German alpine horns and (right bottom) Italian dancers in World Showcase. Left: the Hôtel du Canada, (top) Chinese dancers, (above) Italian pageantry and (facing page) Moroccan music and bright, authentic Moroccan costumes, World Showcase.

27

Great care has been taken to ensure that the styles of architecture, cuisine and entertainment in each of the pavilions in the World Showcase (these pages) correspond closely to their originals. The goods on sale were almost all made in the appropriate country, and the majority of staff are native to the land which they help to evoke. Above: French chef Micky poses beside the real thing, backed by the mansard roof and casement windows of the superb Chefs de France restaurant in the French pavilion. Still in France, Goofy the Scottish Highlander is sketched by a Parisian street artist (right). Far right: German dancing and (facing page) salutes from a beefeater and a Highland soldier outside the Toy Soldier, where traditional British toys are sold.

29

These pages: World Showcase. Right: the Japanese pagoda, on World Showcase Promenade, modeled after an eighth-century structure in the Horyuji Temple in Nara. Below: the Italian pavilion's scaled-down version of the Campanile of St. Mark's in Venice. The gold-leafed angel at its top, together with the statues of St. Mark the Evangelist and the lion, the protector of Venice, are all accurately sculpted after their originals. Below right: a good British-brewed pint in the United Kingdom pavilion's Rose and Crown Pub, and (facing page bottom) German beer in the lively Biergarten. Facing page top: a belly dancer provides exotic mealtime entertainment in Morocco's Marrakesh restaurant in World Showcase. Overleaf: (left top) Donald and friends career down Main Street, U.S.A. on the old time scarlet fire engine and (left bottom) Alice, the Walrus and the White Rabbit greet visitors to Fantasyland's Mad Tea Party ride, all in the Magic Kingdom. Overleaf right: Mickey and Minnie out for a stroll.

The show in the stunning, silver geosphere of Spaceship Earth (left, top and facing page top) examines the history and future of human communications. Above: the wheel-shaped World of Motion, and (facing page bottom) the glass pyramids of the Journey into Imagination, EPCOT Center. Overleaf: smiles for the camera.

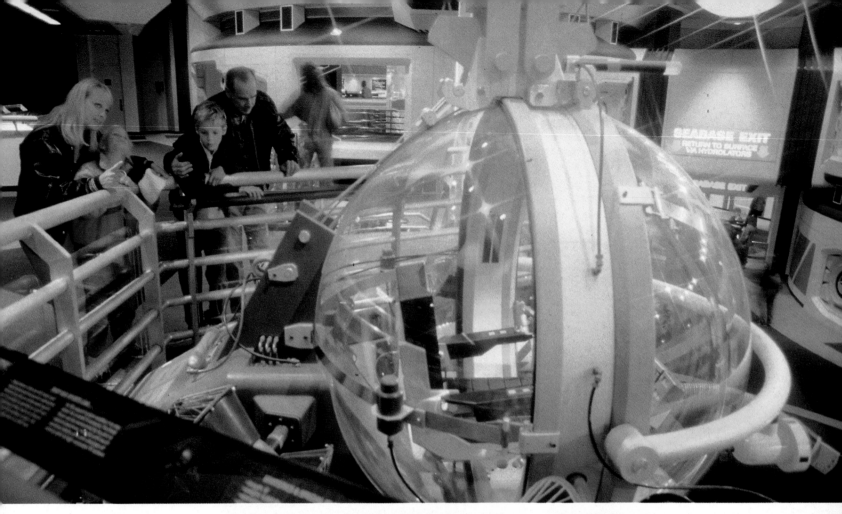

In the Living Seas pavilion (these pages, overleaf and following pages) visitors take a simulated journey deep under the sea, and then travel along a man-made coral reef on the Caribbean Coral Reef Ride. The reef, set in a 5.7 million gallon tank, faithfully reproduces ecosystems found in the Caribbean sea and is stocked with appropriate reef vegetation and over 200 varieties of the sealife which would naturally inhabit such an environment. Among these are butterfly fish and the delicate angelfish, parrot fish, barracuda, sharks, dolphins and sea lions. In this setting, scuba divers demonstrate the most recent advances in diving equipment and underwater monitoring devices, answering visitors' questions via radio links as they do so. Above: a full-size reproduction of the Deep Rover, a one-man submersible vehicle, in Seabase Concourse. Following pages left bottom: fresh seafood in the Coral Reef Restaurant.

THE LIVING SEAS

PRESENTED BY

UNITED TECHNOLOGIES

Within the Magic Kingdom are six distinct lands, each with its own meticulously-sustained theme and atmosphere. In Old-West-style Frontierland, the Country Bear Vacation Hoedown (previous pages) is held in Grizzly Hall and stars a company of life-size Audio-Animatronics bears, each with its own colorful character and musical contribution. Big Thunder Mountain Railroad (bottom left) hurtles through Frontierland's Wild West, while an old-fashioned omnibus (left) and a horse-drawn trolley (facing page top) provide appropriate transport on the Magic Kingdom's version of the typical turn-of-the-century small-town main street, Main Street, U.S.A. Below: the *Empress Lilly* in Walt Disney World Village, and (facing page bottom) the Epcot Center's World of Motion Show. Overleaf: (left top) River Country, (left bottom) the Jungle Cruise in Adventureland and (right) Spaceship Earth.

The Main Street Electrical Parade (these pages), presented only in busy seasons, provides a dazzling spectacle for the gathered crowds. Around 100 performers and nearly 30 floats, decked out in a million points of colored light, parade down Main Street and around Town Square to the lively accompaniment of the "Baroque Hoedown" by Gershon Kingsley and Jean-Jacques Perrey. Below: Goofy and Mickey, (right) Pete atop his dragon and (remaining pictures) Cinderellas. Overleaf: magic fireworks.

64

On the six acres of the Land pavilion (these pages), in the EPCOT Center's Future World, the subject of discovery is food – its production and nutritional value. The Listen to the Land boat ride explores the history and possible future (facing page top and below) of farming, while the Tomorrow's Harvest Tour explains to visitors the experimental agricultural techniques being put into practice in the pavilion and nearby greenhouses. Facing page bottom: Mr. Broccoli and associates, stars of the Kitchen Kabaret, which deals, loosely, with nutrition. Overleaf: Easter parade.

73

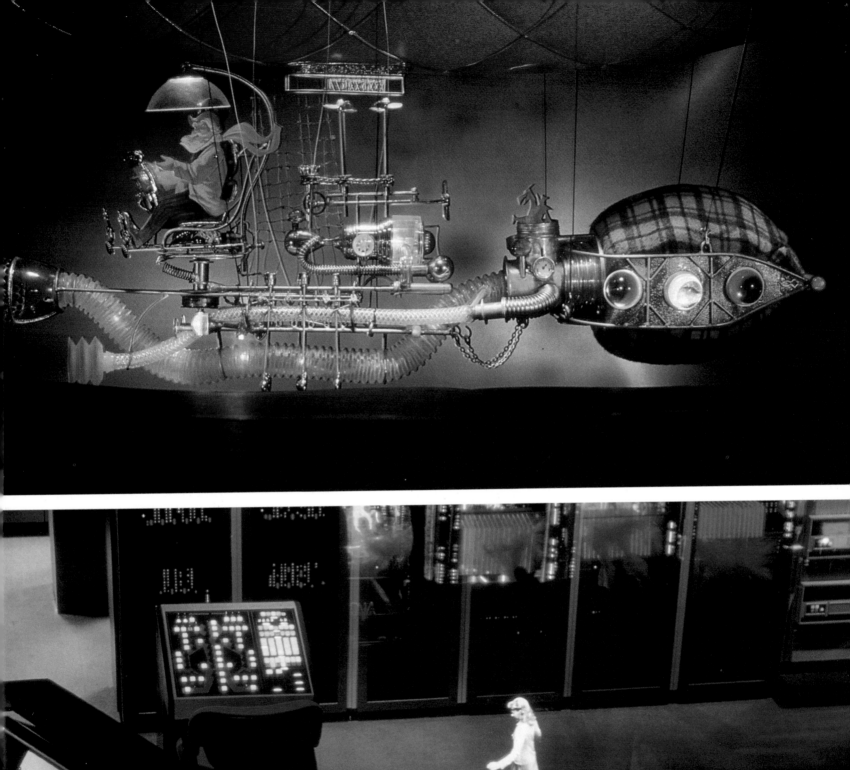

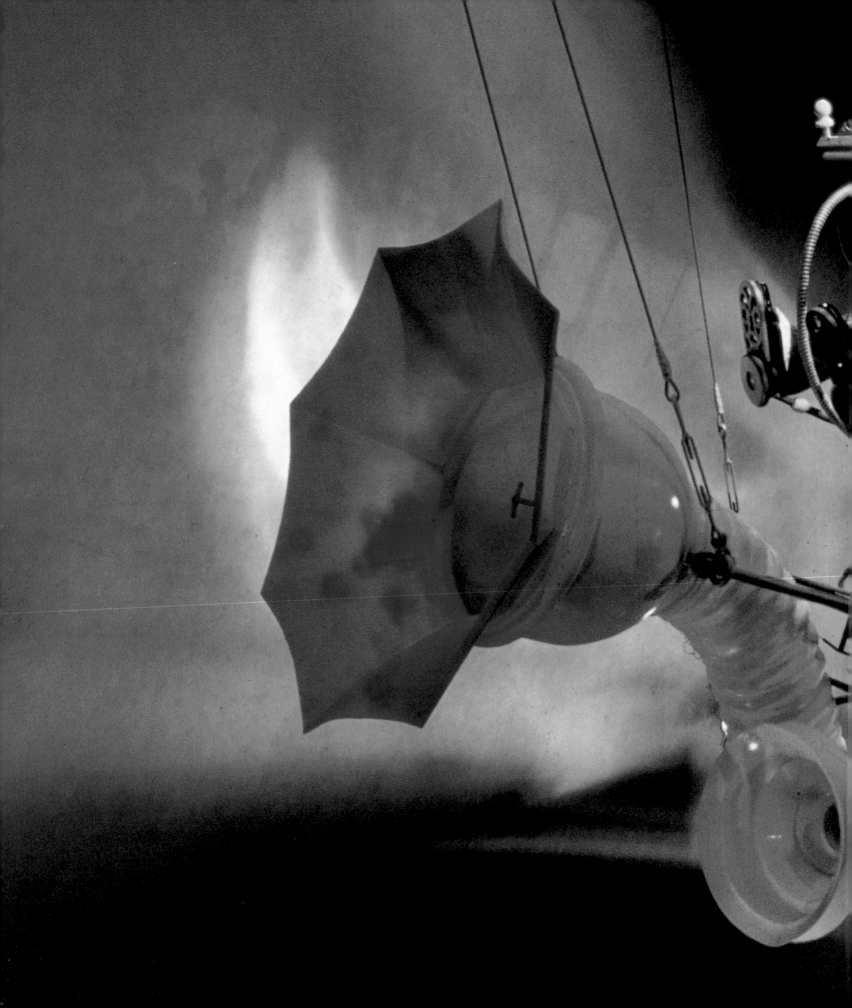